REDU WELLNESS CENTER

USUI REIKI RYOHO

LEVEL 3

CERTIFICATION MANUAL

ENERGY HEALING FOR MASTER PRACTITIONER

SONYA ROY

USUI REIKI RYOHO

CERTIFICATION MANUAL FOR LEVEL 3

ENERGY HEALING FOR MASTER PRACTITIONER

SONYA ROY

To order additional copies of this book, contact the author or Amazon. You can contact the author through multimedia:

Website: Sonyaroy.com

Email: info@sonyaroy.com

Facebook: www.facebook.com/sonya.roy.author

www.facebook.com/reduwellnesscentre/

Twitter: @RoySonyaroy

Podcast: sonyaroy.podbean.com

Revised date: 2021-08-27

Legal Deposit : Library and Archives Canada

Category : Self-realization (psychology); Mind and Body, Holistic Medicine, Change (Psychology) Biography, Spiritual Transformation

Redu Wellness Center
336 Rue Robert
Ange-Gardien, Québec, Canada, J0E 1 E0
Tel : (450)210-3101

NOTICE TO READERS

The ideas and techniques described in this manual are intended for Reiki students. The ability to receive and give Reiki energy cannot be transmitted without having previously received energy placement or energy attunement by a master teacher.

This attunement may vary depending on the method by which the master teacher received it.

This manual contains all the information necessary to cover the Reiki level 3. This Manual is perfect to be used in a training course by a master teacher.

The author of this book does not give medical advice or recommend the use of techniques as a form of treatment for physical, emotional or medical problems without the advice of a doctor, whether directly or indirectly. The author's goal is only to provide general information to assist you in your quest for emotional and spiritual well-being. In the event that you use any of the information in this book for yourself, which is your constitutional right, the author and the publisher assume no responsibility for your actions.

According to The Canadian Reiki Association everyone who receives and gives Reiki understands the following principle:

- I understand that Reiki is a stress reduction and relaxation technique.
- I acknowledge that sessions administered are only for the purpose of helping me relax and to relieve stress.
- Reiki Practitioners do not diagnose conditions, nor do they prescribe substances or perform medical treatment, nor interfere with the treatment of a licensed medical professional.
- It is recommended that I see a licensed physician, or licensed health care professional for any physical or psychological ailment or condition I may have.

Acknowledgements

I have to thank those who have helped me correct spelling, grammar, and possible mistakes that sometimes creep in when composing a book, including Kris Pel and Paula Johnston. I would also like to thank those who encouraged me in this project and who believed in me. Thank you so much!

TABLE OF CONTENTS

Schedule

09:00   Introduction of each participant

09:15   Review what we are learning today in our 7 hour class and distribute the professional grade Reiki Level 3 manual to each student.

9:30   Master Practitioner attunement

10:00   The master symbol (Usui DAI KO MYO)

10:15   Review of the level 1 & 2 Usui Reiki:

- ❖ History of Reiki   5 principle of Reiki   History
- ❖ Effects of reiki   Symbols CKR, SHK,HSZSN

11:00   Aura clearing techniques and cutting Psychic cords

12:00   LUNCH

13:00   The Crystal Grid with Reiki

13:45   Sacred Geometry

14:00   Explanation of a Reiki table session and the integration of the Master Symbol

14:15   Reiki table session

15:30   Reiki table session (change of partner)

16:30   Canadian Reiki Association Criteria

17:00   Reiki Master Practitioner Certificate + Homework

INTRODUCTION

I would like to congratulate you on your decision to continue your journey on the road of Reiki. The Master Practitioner level allows you to obtain the master symbol and give even more powerful Reiki.

The development of our ability to give Reiki to someone varies with our ability to enlarge our central channel of energy. Imagine that at the start you have a small fire and you want to put it out so you bring with you a bucket of water that you throw over the fire and the fire is mastered. This is the equivalent of Reiki at the first level. At level two you now have access to a garden hose and since you have access to more water, less effort is required to get water from one place to another. You can also water your lawn without having to be present with long distance Reiki. But if you're trying to manage a burning house with a garden hose, the process can be long.

With the placement of the master symbol, we can now compare the central energy channel to the fire hose. Since the hose is much larger, more water is used to control the fire and put it out. You now have access to a greater capacity to deliver a greater volume of Reiki during the same period of time.

Our daily meditation practice continues and evolves. The sensitivity of our hands to recognize the energy that varies according to the symbol used is developing and facilitating the use of the Byosen sweeping method.

With the Master Practitioner level we will learn to work to incorporate the Master Symbol during our Reiki table session as well as in a new procedure called aura cleansing.

At this level, we also learn to use the resources around us, such as crystals, to help us amplify our energy. Crystals are more than objects shaped long ago, they have a consciousness that allows them to make a connection with us. This connection helps us form a work team and amplify our intentions, focusing that excess energy to work on a cause or release a blockage.

We deepen our knowledge of the universe and incorporate the science of sacred geometry into the development of our crystal grids. The grid then becomes our assistant in our daily energy production and helps us do more work at the same time.

I should note that the master practitioner level does not entitle you to teach Reiki to other people. This privilege comes with the teachings received at the Master Teacher level.

REVIEW OF THE REIKI HISTORY

MIKAO USUI

In the original oral tradition of Reiki classes, information was diluted and sometimes altered. We are now using the information which is inscribed on the commemorative stele of Usui, in Japan.

Mikao Usui, Sensei, the founder and the teacher of Reiki, was born in 1865 in the village of Taniai in the district of Yamagata in the prefecture of Gifu, located near the current site of Nagoya in Japan. He was a very spiritual man - a man who took his daily exercises in religion and meditation very seriously.

He lived in difficult conditions during his childhood, he was a good student and his skills were superior to his friends. As an adult, he traveled to Europe, America and also studied in China. He was trained in medicine, psychology, religion and the art of divination. He belonged to a metaphysical group called Rei Jyutu Ka, which aimed to develop parapsychological skills.

He had several jobs of all kinds. He was a civil servant, company employee and journalist, and helped in the reintegration of detainees. He was also the secretary of Shinpei Goto, of the Ministry of Health and Welfare.

He then directed his time and efforts to reach a special state of consciousness called An-shin Ritus-Mei, which translates to finding inner peace. The phenomenon can also be named by witnessing it or being in the neutral positive. In this state of consciousness, a person can accomplish the purpose of his soul. He managed to find a teacher who could help him enter and stay in this state through Zazen meditation, but his efforts remained unsuccessful after 3 years.

His teacher suggested a more rigorous state of meditation which required the person to be ready to die to find this state, and so in March 1922 Usui Sensei climbed Mount Kurama near a small waterfall where he meditated while fasting. Sensei may have sat under the waterfall to let the water hit the top of his head to open his crown chakra. After 21 days of fasting and meditation he felt tired, weak and close to death. Thanks to his deep devotion, his vast personal research and his life experiences, he was awakened to an even more targeted energy transfer that is described as a powerful bright energy, that struck him like lightning and he lost consciousness. This energy is now known as Reiki.

When he woke up at sunrise, he felt that he was filled with a vitality of peace and energy. He had successfully raised his level of consciousness and finally achieved his new state of enlightenment. So excited by this event, he ran down the mountain and hit his toe on a rock and fell. He did what we all do when we get hurt, he put his hands on his toe.

It is then that Usui Sensei experienced the first of 4 miracles.

1) Healing energy began to flow from his hands and healed his injured toe.

2) At the bottom of the mountain, he entered a restaurant and ordered a large meal and can eat it without being sick even though he had fasted for 21 days.

3) The waitress who served him had a stomach ache and he touched her with his hands and she was cured.

4) He returned to the monastery where one of the old monks suffered from terrible arthritis. He fell asleep and Dr. USUI put his hands on him and relieved his pain.

He tried it on himself and on family members, it had immediate results. He realized that it was better to spread this power widely among the world for all to benefit from it rather than to keep it exclusively for family members. He named his method: Shin-Shin Kai-Zen Usui Reiki Ryo-ho which translates to the Reiki Usui treatment method for the improvement of body and mind. This name is simplified as Usui Reiki Ryo-ho. Reiki is not an invention of Mikao Usui as there were other methods of energy transfer that existed at the time.

Matiji Kawakami was a Japanese therapist who created Reiki Ryoho, and in 1919 published a book called Reiki Ryoho to Sono Koka. The Reikan Tonetsu Ryoho was created by Reikaku Ishinuki. The Senshinryu Reiki Ryoho was created by Kogetsu Matsubara and the Seido Reishojutsu was created by Reisen Oyama.

What does this mean? It is clear that energy healing is thousands of years old and is not necessarily from Japan. However, in Japan, any system that works with energy is called Reiki.

Dr. USUI began healing the poor people in Japan but he saw that the people he had healed and who had found a job had become beggars again. They told him that they did not really want to be cured and that they were happy not to work and to beg for a living. Dr. Usui realized that not everyone wants to be cured. So, at that time, he changed his goal of healing the poor to healing those who came to him asking for healing. Set up a Reiki practice and a school.

Mikao Usui moved to Tokyo in April 1922 and established an institute where the REIKI system is taught to the public and treatments were also given. He also opened clinics in Harajuku and Aoyama and people came from all over to seek healing.

In September 1923, Tokyo had a big fire due to an earthquake in the Kanto district. Mikao Usui was dedicated to helping the many injured and affected people. He later received a medal for his efforts.

Master Usui had nearly 2,000 students of various skill and dedication levels who had learned meditation in groups across Japan, mainly in the Tokyo area.

The earthquake and the resulting tsunami and fire had caused such great demand for healers that Mikao Usui began to train teachers so that they in turn could teach more than one person to help more people. It was while developing his Reiki system that he included the 3 symbols called Okuden as well as a new, more formal attunement process called Reiju kai. He also added the three pillar method: Gassho, Reiji-ho and Chiryo as well as Byosen Scanning, and other methods such as Gyoshi ho and Seishin-to-itsu.

The first pillar is the Gassho. We join hands in prayer and repeat the 5 principles of Reiki.

The second pillar, Reiji-ho, means the indication of the spirit. This method uses intuition to put the hands in the right place and helps us to determine how to do a session.

The third pillar is the Chiryo which means treatment. Usui taught his students to follow their own inner guide rather than a set of pre-determined hand positions.

Among the 20 teachers trained by Mikao Usui were Toshihiro Eguchi, Jusaburo Guida, Kan'ichi Taketomi, Toyoichi Wanami, Yoshiharu Watanabe, Keizo Ogawa, J. Ushida and Chujiro Hayashi.

Mikao Usui used only 1 type of attunement which he repeated several times to the same person. He taught that a student should receive as much attunement as possible to increase and refine the quality of their Reiki energy. There weren't different attunements for each level and no specific attunement to activate the symbols.

His training center became too small to receive all of the visitors, so he built a new house in Nakano in February 1925.

With his reputation growing, Mikao Usui was invited to travel across the country. He went to Kure, Hiroshima, Saga and Fukuyama. It was at the inn on the road to Fukuyama that he fell ill and died on March 9, 1926, at the age of 62.

After his death, it was J. Ushida who took the presidency of Usui Reiki Ryoho Gakkai. He was followed by Mr. Llichi Taketomi, Mr. Yoshiharu Watanabe, Mr. Toyoichi Wanami, Miss Kimiko Koyama and the president in 1998 was Mr. Mahayoshi Kondo. There is no grandmaster but a president in charge of the clinics. The first 4 presidents had been trained directly by Mikao Usui Sensei.

The stele that marks his grave at the Saihoji temple in Sugunami, Tokyo indicates that Mikao Usui was a man of a gentle and reasoned temperament that did not care about appearances. He was in good physical shape, robust and always smiling. He loved to read and his knowledge included history, Christian and Buddhist theology, medical sciences, psychology, and even magic, divinatory art and physiognomy.

The author of the information on the stele is Juzaburo Usuhida 4th junior rank, 4th service class, Rear Admiral and was edited by Masayuki Okada 3rd junior rank, 3rd order of merit, doctor of literature.

Juzaburo Usuhida believed that if we can successfully take the Reiki healing system around the world it will eventually affect the moral code of society and he encouraged us to take over the system so that everyone can access it.

Mikao Usui called the first degree or level 1 Shoden. In Shoden there were 4 levels:

- Loku-Tou
- Go-Tou
- Yon-Tou
- San-Tou

Takata, whom we will learn more about later, combined its four levels into one when teaching and Mikao Usui originally gave 4 initiations, but we have now also combined these into one.

The second degree was called Okuden which means interior teaching and contained 2 levels:

- Okuden-Zen-Ki
- Okuden-Koe-Ki

The third degree was called Shinpiden which means Mystery Teaching and represents the master level and includes:

- Shihan-Kaku (assistant teacher)
- Shishan. (venerable teacher)

Mikao Usui used only 3 symbols, he taught them at level 2. This was confirmed by Hiroshi Doi, Hyakuten Inamoto, Arjava Petter and Tadao Yamaguchi.

Western-style Reiki is both practical (healing by the hands) and spiritual (oriented toward mediation) - developed on some of the fundamental principles of Reiki taught by Master Usui - but not entirely. Due to the different nature of our culture and the times, his classes were entirely different - so there are no "traditional" Usui-type courses taught in North America and probably not in Japan. His courses were undertaken with long-term commitments, which we do not require in the West. Even though we often read that someone teaches in the same way as Master Usui, we doubt that the student registered for an unlimited number of years - one evening per week.

What we do know is that the course content may have similarities and overlaps and that the method of energy transmission and healing concepts may also be somewhat similar.

We also know that Master Usui met like-minded people and that information was shared by others who had perfected similar skills. Master Usui had an open mind and a big heart. Master

Usui had an open mind and a big heart, hence the idea of sharing information and inviting other healers among them, then incorporating some of the concepts he deemed appropriate so that Reiki would evolve. Thus, energy work is still evolving today.

Before he died, he asked Dr. Hayashi Sensei, a retired naval medical officer, to open his own clinic and continue to develop Reiki based on his medical knowledge, thus continuing the practice that Dr. USUI had started.

DR. HAYASHI

Known in the west as Master Chujiro Hayashi, he was a devoted student who was taught by Master Usui. He became master (Shinpiden) in 1925 when he was 46 years old.

Hayashi kept notes on the medical conditions of his patients and the position of the hands that gave the best results. This led him to create Reiki Ryoho Shinshin, which translates to Guidelines for the Reiki Healing Method. This manual was distributed to his students and was only to be used if the practitioner was not able to use the Byosen to scan for the best positions of the hands. To make use of it, we must have an accurate diagnosis to make use of the method limited to this health problem. Since we are not doctors and therefore cannot make a diagnosis, this manual is no longer used. We also recognize from Hayashi the basic hand position method that is eventually taught by Mrs. Takata.

Dr Hayashi also changed the way we give Reiki. Mikao Usui would give Reiki on a chair and take care of one person at a time. Hayashi gave his treatment while the person was lying on a table and could receive Reiki from several people at the same time.

He also changed the attunement to make the method more efficient and developed a new way of teaching while traveling. With this new method he taught level 1 and 2 together for 5 days. Each day included an attunement and 2 to 3 hours of instruction. He trained 13 masters, including Mrs. Hawayo Takata.

He made a trip to Hawaii in 1937-38 to help Mrs. Takata develop her own clinic. Upon his return to Japan, he was interrogated by the military who wanted to obtain information on potential targets in Honolulu to plan their attack on Pearl Harbor. He refused to cooperate and was declared a traitor. Following Japanese tradition, he and his family would be dishonoured and ostracized by Japanese society. Instead he decided to die honourably by a ritual suicide called seppuku on May 11, 1940.

MRS HAWAYO TAKATA

The Hayashi Reiki teaching line reached the west through Master Hawayo Takata. Although it is the best known and most prolific, it is not the only line, nor the only source of original information that Master Usui disseminated and used.

Ms. Hawayo Takata herself summed up her life before her first contact with Dr. Hayashi's clinic. She was born on December 24, 1900 in Kauai, Hawaii. Her parents were Japanese immigrants and her father worked on the sugar plantations. She married the plantation accountant named Saichi Takata and they had 2 daughters.

In October 1930, Saichi Takata died at the age of 34 and left Hawayo alone. She had to start working in order to provide for them and after 5 years developed severe abdominal problems and a pulmonary condition and she sank into depression.

Takata had to travel to Japan around 1936 to announce the death of her sister to her parents who had returned to live there. Once there, she went to the hospital for diagnosis and help. She was diagnosed with a tumor, gall stones, appendicitis and asthma and would require surgery. She went to the Hayashi clinic for a second opinion. She was impressed that the diagnosis matched that which she had received at the hospital and decided to get treatment at the Hayashi clinic. She received 1 treatment per day by 2 practitioners. She remembered that the heat in their hands was so strong that she believed they were secretly using instruments hidden in the sleeves of their kimono to create heat. She tried unsuccessfully to find the instruments and that is when she learned about Reiki and how it works. She got progressively better and healed in 4 months.

In the spring of 1936, she began to learn Reiki with Dr. Hayashi. She worked with him for 1 year and received the second degree of Reiki. She returned to Hawaii in 1937 where Dr. Hayashi came to help her open her clinic with her daughter. On February 21, 1938, Hayashi initiated Ms. Takata to master level.

She was very successful in Hawaii and traveled elsewhere in the United States and Canada to teach Reiki until her death on December 11, 1980. It is thanks to her that Reiki came out of Japan and is now practiced by more than a million people around the world. She often taught Reiki to the family member of the patient she was treating so that they, too, could give Reiki to speed healing. Her treatments could last for hours.

She started initiating masters only after the year 1970. She would charge $10,000 for a reiki master's degree for training that only lasted one weekend. These raised fees were not part of the Reiki system.

She believed that you should never teach or give treatment for free, that there should always be an exchange. She insisted that there should be only one master teacher and that reiki was an oral tradition and should be learned by heart without taking notes or writing symbols. After consulting other Reiki groups in Japan, though, we find that she no doubt created this it is a rule and that even Hayashi gave a textbook to his students.

Comparing notes several years later that some of Master Takata's students had taken after the course ended, we can see variations between students. This shows that even with energetic healing work, it has been fluid.

The emphasis was not placed on the advanced development of intuition as in the first classes of Mikao Usui. But followed a simplified method of Dr. Hayashi. Master Takata, who was probably the first to teach Reiki in the Western world, taught her level one student 8 separate hand positions so that anyone could practice Reiki. She called her 8 hand positions the "basic treatment."

She is credited with the different attunements at each level as well as the elimination of typical Japanese Reiki techniques and the addition of the master symbol which was not taught until now.

Takata initiated 22 masters. Before her death, she told her masters that she had made no changes to the way that Reiki was taught and assured them that she was the only living Reiki master in the world following the Second World War. They swore a solemn oath that they would not change the way Reiki was taught.

Meanwhile in Japan, Reiki was practiced in secret after the Second World War. The United States controlled Japan and prohibited any form of Japanese treatment unless an application was made and approved and Reiki fells into the shadows.

IRIS ISHIKURA

Iris Ishikura had training as a healer with the Johrei Fellowship, which promoted healing by the projection of energy by the hands, in addition to Reiki training with Mrs. Takata.

She also underwent energy healing training from her sister who worked in a Tibetan temple in Hawaii. Following the death of Takata Sensei, she trained 2 Reiki masters. Out of respect for her, she waited until then to lower the cost of training to make it more available to everyone.

One of the masters was her daughter Ruby who did not teach Reiki and the other was Arthur Robertson

It was Iris and those trained by the other Takata masters who were guided by their wisdom and knowledge to practice and teach Reiki. It was also at this time that the master level was split in two: The master practitioner level, which contains information on the master symbol, crystals, aura operations, and the master teacher level, which contains the attunement to initiate students and the right to be a teacher.

This is where Reiki textbooks were created, reasonable fees were fixed, course notes were allowed and a student could choose to work with more than one teacher. With decreased costs, reiki has grown exponentially around the world.

ARTHUR ROBERTSON

Arthur Robertson was also a teacher of Tibetan Shamanism, a method that included several symbols as well as an attunement technique called the transmission of power. This method was similar to Usui's Reiki method and he fused the two methods into one new one. The new method included 2 Tibetan symbols and the Purple Breath as well as the integration of the 3 Okuden symbols of the Usui Reiki system which developed the Usui Reiki / Tibetan model.

MASTER SYMBOL

The master symbol used in Usui Ryoho's system is simply the word Dai Ko Myo written in Kanji, the form of Japanese writing. As it is not a SYMBOL but a writing, like any form of writing there are many variations. I have added a few examples below to help students realize that the form taught depends on the lineage from which it comes. There is no perfect form, but there is a perfect writing of the word DAI KO MYO. All the variations that exist come from there.

The meaning of Dai Ko Myo is difficult to translate because the Kanji symbols can have multiple translations and the combination of the drawings then give a meaning other than the original words.

DAI can mean   a) a human with extended arms and legs.
                  b) neglect or close your eyes
                  c) a flood
KO can mean   a) light, ray
                  b) sunlight, sunshine
                  c) radiate light, emit light
                  d) a torch carried by a human
MYO can mean   a) dawn
                  b) tomorrow
                  c) cross the night towards dawn

In the context of Reiki, Dai Ko Myo is translated as "great being of the universe, shine on me, bring me to the light".

The Encyclopedia of Eastern Philosophy and Religion lists a definition of this symbol as "the treasure of the great radiant light" and explains that it is "A Zen expression of one's own true nature as being Buddha, which one becomes aware in the experience of enlightenment."

The master symbol is used to increase the connection between the physical body and the higher self, thus bringing wisdom and greater power into the vessel body. For a person to benefit from Reiki they must take responsibility for their actions which have caused the imbalances in the physical body that are causing health problems. Dai Ko Myo helps a person to glimpse their true divine nature and thus encourage them to change their behavior and live in a healthier way. This divine wisdom influences a person, through Reiki, to show more self-respect, to eat better, to do light exercises, and to recognize the holiness of their body.

Dai Ko Myo increases the value of other symbols because it connects and activates energies to work together for the betterment of the person.

Dai Ko Myo like all other symbols can be used to purify objects and food or help focus during meditation. In a Reiki session, it can be incorporated at any time. You can call on Dai Ko Myo according to your intuition or follow a more specific method presented during the explanations for a table session.

The element associated with it is ether and the associated color is purple or white.
The abbreviation for Dai Ko Myo is UDKM to differentiate Kanji from the Tibetan symbol of the same name. The alternate name of the symbol is the master symbol.

To activate this energy you can simply:
Draw the symbol above the space or object where you want to send energy or imagine the symbol there and then say three times aloud or silently: Dai Ko Myo

This is the written version of Dai Ko Myo :

Here are examples of different ways of teaching to draw the symbol, and we'll focus on just one method on the next page:

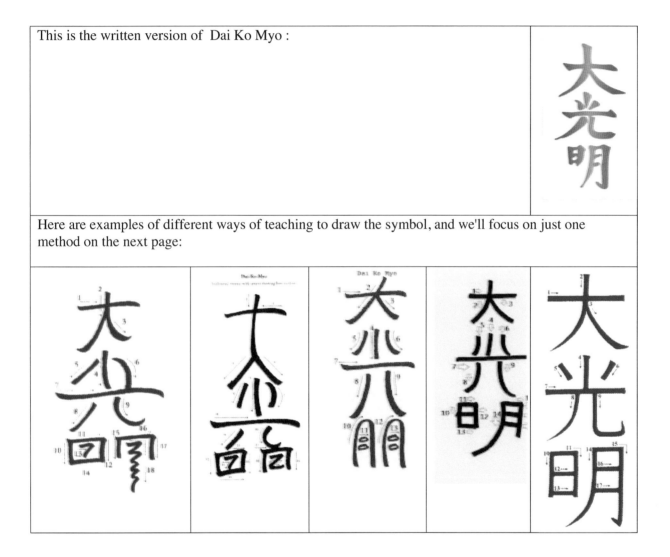

DAI KO MYO

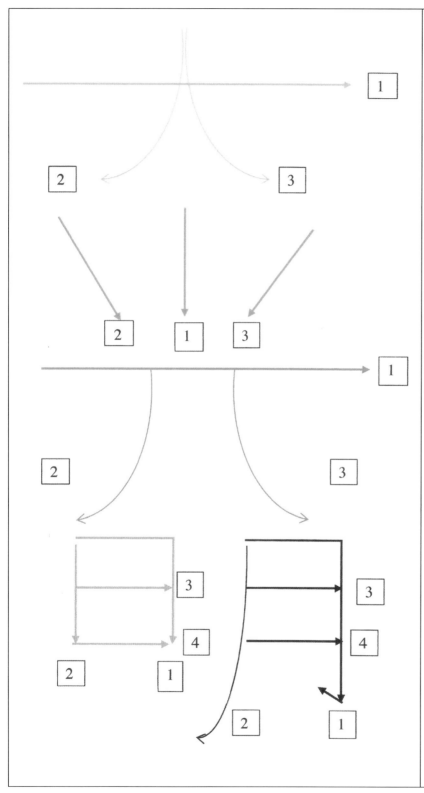

1. Line 1 is drawn from left to right.

2. We draw the curved line from top to bottom to the left

3. We draw the curved line from top to bottom to the right

4. Draw the central line first and then the 2 lines on each side

5. We draw the line from left to right first and then the 2 legs, left first and right second.

6. Draw each box the same way, the first line starts at the top and ends in the bottom right corner. The second line forms the left side. The third line is the middle bar and the last line forms the base of the box.

The second box has lines that go beyond the box.

After the drawing is finished, the symbol is activated by saying its name 3 times: DAI KO MYO

ATTUNEMENT

The Dai Ko Myo symbol is received during the third level attunement. We can expect a more heightened experience of the energies, mainly because our central channel was opened and subsequently, we did 21 days of morning meditation to incorporate these energies into us and heal ourselves. At level 2, we did 40 days of meditation and self-healing and as a result we developed our sensitivity to energy and symbols. A 6 month period has now passed and you should have completed at least 24 case studies in order to familiarize yourself with Reiki sessions and be comfortable giving them. Every time you give Reiki to someone else, you yourself are receiving Reiki, which helps you stay connected and receive a greater volume of energy.

This experience is personal to each, but in general whatever your experience may be at other levels will be amplified. It is all the more plausible that your senses are also more aroused and you could finally see colors, hear sounds, see energy lines or a person. Sensations are also related to the gifts of clairsentience. The more you work with Reiki the more your senses will develop and the more you will be guided.

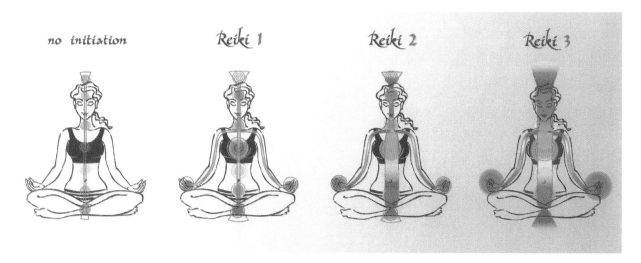

It also goes without saying that your preparation influences your body. At Level 2, we had recommendations to follow to prepare for harmonization. Why should people stop drinking coffee or alcohol or stop smoking? For several reasons, the first being that most of the things that are suggested to be avoided are stimulants to the body. If you regularly consume these ingredients, your body is constantly in a state of hyper-stimulation. This affects your ability to sense energy and your non-physical bodies (Emotional, Mental, Spiritual and Etheric).

The second reason is that you are using these things in order to avoid dealing with what is happening with your other bodies. By desensitizing yourself, you do not see the information you have to deal with that comes from these bodies. For example, someone who eats their emotions rarely does so with pieces of carrots and celery. They choose foods that create a chemical reaction similar to the emotion they desire. By eliminating these products from your lifestyle, you will finally be able to access blockages and Reiki is then a great way to free yourself.

It is therefore up to you to choose what you can do to be as well prepared as possible for your harmonization. The best preparation is to follow all the tips and then ask yourself if you really need to go back or continue with the changes made.

PREPARATION FOR AN ATTUNEMENT

1. Limit or cut out animal protein for the 3 days prior. Fish is fine. This is to clear negative energies from food.
2. If you have ever fasted and enjoy this process, fasting on juice or water beforehand is good. (1-2 days or just a few hours). If you are not used to this then just try to eat healthy.
3. Limit or stop any caffeinated drinks for 3 days.
4. Limit or no alcohol for 3 days.
5. Limit or no sugar or junk food for 3 days.
6. Limit or stop smoking cigarettes for 3 days.
7. Quiet negative outside distractions such as news, horror movies, etc for 3 days.
8. Try to spend some time appreciating nature each day.
9. Start as soon as possible to meditate daily, an hour if possible. If you are not able to meditate, just sit quietly and contemplate. Ask to release anger, fear, worry, and other negative feelings. Then spend some time contemplating or meditating on why you want to receive a Reiki Attunement and what you wish to receive from your Reiki Attunement. (e.g to increase your psychic ability or to be able to heal yourself and others, mentally and physically, etc.)
10. If you use other rituals or methods to get your psychic powers stimulated, go ahead and start preparing yourself. (e.g. Crystals, candles...)

Again, many people do nothing beforehand, so do not stress about this, but a quiet contemplating period before would be good. At the very least, avoid a heavy party weekend.

HOMEWORK AND PRACTICE

Meditation for 30 days

Start meditation with your Master crystal

1. Draw USUI DKM using the whole hand (purple)

2. Hold the imaginary image in front of you and say 3 times Dai Ko Myo

3. Meditate holding the imaginary image for several minutes up to 10 minutes creating an energy bubble containing the symbol Dai Ko Myo

4. Move the bubble above your head

5. Repeat steps 2 to 5 with Cho Ku Rei

6. Repeat steps 2 to 5 with Sei Hi Ki

7. Repeat steps 2 to 5 with Hon Sha Ze Sho Nen

8. Imagine the bubbles above your head descending around you and being absorbed into you, one by one.

9. You can do this for your convenience or specify an "I want to heal..." goal.

10. Say, "If it is possible according to divine will, divine wisdom and divine love, then so be it."

11. Visualize this for about 10 minutes, let the energy activate within you.

12. Load your REIKI grid with the master crystal, if necessary

13. Close your REIKI

REIKI CRYSTAL GRID

Choosing the right crystals:

1. Quartz crystal has the unique ability of being able to absorb desire and intentions, they can be chosen using the following methods:

 a. Use a pendulum

 b. Byosen

 c. Muscle tests

2. How to clean crystals after buying or using them:

 a. Brush them with a toothbrush

 b. Wash them under running water or simply wash them with a mild detergent

 c. A mantra or song

 d. In the light of the full moon

 e. Smudge with sage

 f. Use Reiki energy and the Dai Ko Myo symbol

 g. The vibration of drums, Tibetan bowls or other crystals.

 h. Be careful, salt can damage your crystals. The sun may affect the coloring of some crystals, it is better not to put the crystals under direct sunlight

3. You can use the crystals on the chakras during a session.

Crystals are living things. They speak intuitively and we can converse with them. However, since you cannot really communicate with a baby, it is difficult to communicate with some crystals. Take the time to try, starting with a larger crystal that has had time to grow, evolve, and develop its ability to communicate with other conscious beings. As sentient beings, crystals do not belong to the person buying them. They are the gift of mother earth and should be cherished and given freely. The only exception is a crystal of life, these crystals are linked to a person and work with them closely during their present incarnation. Crystals will appear and disappear all the time. When they disappear, it is to be recharged by Elementals. Just give them time to reappear once recharged.

I give all of my students a master crystal with which they start working with from level 1. They use their master crystal during their meditation to establish a personal connection with it. Now the crystal is ready to work with you to energize your crystal grid. At level 2, with the help of HSZSN, we learned how to store energy inside a crystal for later use. Now we are going to learn how to generate energy for a person or a cause.

A Grid is based on sacred geometry. The seed of life or the flower are examples explored in the next chapter. After selecting the shape on which you will build your grid, follow the steps below.

Create a grid to send continuous energy to a person or cause for 30 days. Please note that it is important to respect the crystals and let them be energized for a period of 30 days in the earth and then purified in the light of the moon after use. You can have several crystals and build a grid each month alternating groups of crystals to give them time to rest.

Depending on your grid a certain number of crystals are necessary. For the seed of life, the example shown below, choose 8 clear quartz crystals.

Place either a double tip, pyramid, crystal ball, or crystal cluster in the center of the grid. Under the central crystal, place either a photo or write the name of the person or cause that will receive the energy from the grid. For example, you are sending energy to your kidneys or to cure rheumatism or to sell your house.

Place the crystals on the conjuncture of the lines of the sacred geometric shape. Place the points towards the center. Once all the crystals are placed make sure that your master crystal is loaded. The master crystal is charged by meditating with it for 30 minutes.

Make sure your Reiki is on and point the master crystal at the center and form the first triangle saying "I load this grid with REIKI, with REIKI, with REIKI, for..." Here are some examples for which you can use your grid:

a) I load this grid with REIKI, with REIKI, with REIKI, for love, for love, for love

b) I load this grid with REIKI, with REIKI, with REIKI for health, for health, for health

c) For Joy, for peace, for wisdom, for abundance

You can load a grid for love, prosperity, joy but try to keep the crystals evenly distributed. For example, if you have 6 points you can have 6 different intentions, 6 alike, 2 groups of 3, or 3 groups of 2.

You can add other words as you like Health. Or change the phrase to "REIKI for LIGHT" or "I connect this REIKI grid to my higher self to heal myself, heal, heal" or "I connect this grid with the power of GOD to heal to heal to heal." Visualize what you want and meditate on the grid after completing the cycle. You have to load the grid every day.

If you are traveling, bring a photo of the grid and the master crystal with you and load your grid, after meditating, each day.

Identify each junction of the lines to determine the number of crystals needed

Place a crystal on each junction of the lines

Start loading the grid from the center

Then follow the lines that form a piece of pizza

For this example, a petal completes the form

And we return to the center to continue to make the 6 petals

SACRED GEOMETRY

Sacred geometry involves sacred universal patterns used in the design of everything in our reality, most often seen in sacred architecture and sacred art. The fundamental belief is that geometry and mathematical relationships, harmonics and proportions are also found in music, light and cosmology. This value system is considered widespread even in prehistoric times, culturally universal of the human condition.

It is considered fundamental for the construction of sacred structures such as temples, mosques, megaliths, monuments and churches; sacred spaces such as altars and tabernacles; meeting places such as sacred groves, village greens and sacred wells and the creation of religious art, iconography and "divine" proportions. Alternatively, arts based on sacred geometry can be ephemeral, such as visualization, sand painting, and medicine wheels.

Sacred geometry can be understood as a pattern recognition worldview, a complex system of religious symbols and structures involving space, time, and form. According to this view, the basic patterns of existence are seen as sacred. By connecting to these, a believer contemplates the great mysteries and the great design.

THE SPHERE

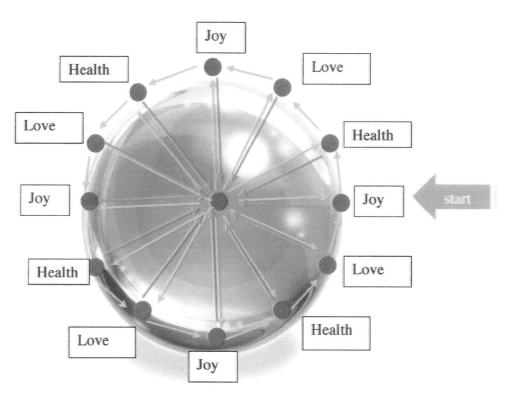

Perhaps one of the simplest and most perfect forms of all, the sphere is an expression of oneness, completeness, integrity and equality. It is the deepest and most sacred symbol in the universe and contains all wisdom of creation.

It is from the sphere that the other forms are organized. With the sphere, we are reminded that everything fits together in perfect proportions and it is the portal that opens you to the workings of nature. One of the best examples of a sphere is Gaia, along with all the other planets. Cells and seeds are also spheres. As a crystal grid, it can be used to unify your aura and energy field. Simply put the crystals all around, as the red dots represent and then put the center piece in the center. You can load the grid clockwise or counter-clockwise, it doesn't matter, only your intention matters.

You start in the center and follow the arrows that form pizza slices and go all the way around. If you have different intentions it is good to write them and stick them near the crystal for a repetition without errors and also to mark your starting point as the arrow indicates.

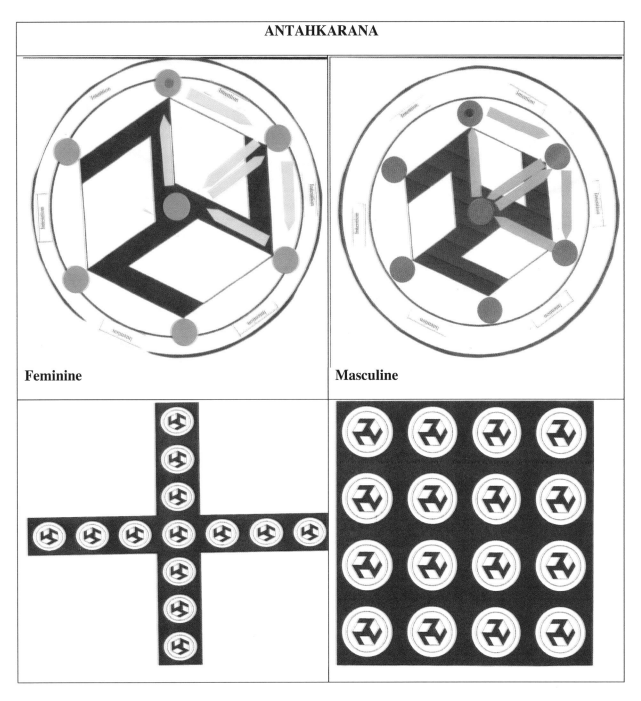

Feminine

Masculine

One of the shapes often used to create crystal grids is the ancient Antahkarana symbol known in Tibet and Egypt. The Antahkarana has two forms, a feminine one which is a slimmer and elongated version which can be used for healing in a gentle way. The male symbol is smaller and thicker and is generally used for more direct, focused and penetrating healing. The two symbols reinforce the intention and make the grid stronger.

You can use sacred geometry on its own or as the basis for a crystal grid.

You can paste the image of your choice under your massage table, or in your workplace. The form releases negative energy, or builds energy at a higher frequency.

THE FLOWER OF LIFE

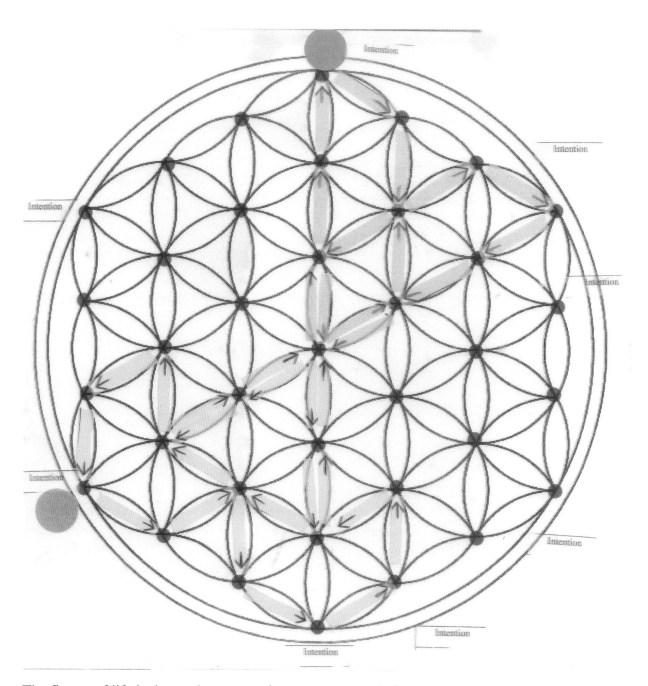

The flower of life is the modern name given to a geometric figure made up of multiple evenly spaced, overlapping circles arranged to form a flower-shaped pattern. The center of each circle is on the circumference of six surrounding circles of the same diameter.

It is considered by some to contain an ancient religious value representing the fundamental forms of space and time. In this sense, it is a visual expression of the connections that life weaves through all sentient beings, believed to contain some type of Akashic record of basic information about all living things.

There are many spiritual beliefs associated with the Flower of Life. For example, representations of the five Platonic solids are found in Metatron's cube symbol, which can be derived from the flower of life model. These Platonic solids are geometric shapes that are said to act as a template from which all life springs. The Flower of Life embodies our life force energy, or Chi, and the life force that flows through us. Our energy, the Earth and everything in the Universe is woven into a common repeating pattern that manifests in the geometry of this one sacred flower. Its perfect and infinite pattern represents the very thread of our being, stretching across planes and dimensions.

The symbol was found at the Temple of Osiris in Abydos, Egypt, the Forbidden City in Beijing, China, and at sacred sites in Israel, India, Spain, and Japan. As a grid it can be used for anything that needs expansion. This shape is very complicated to load, follow the arrows to form the petals shown on the next page. Repeat the blue and orange shapes consecutively until you have gone around the circle. The red dots represent all the places to drop a crystal.

SEED OF LIFE

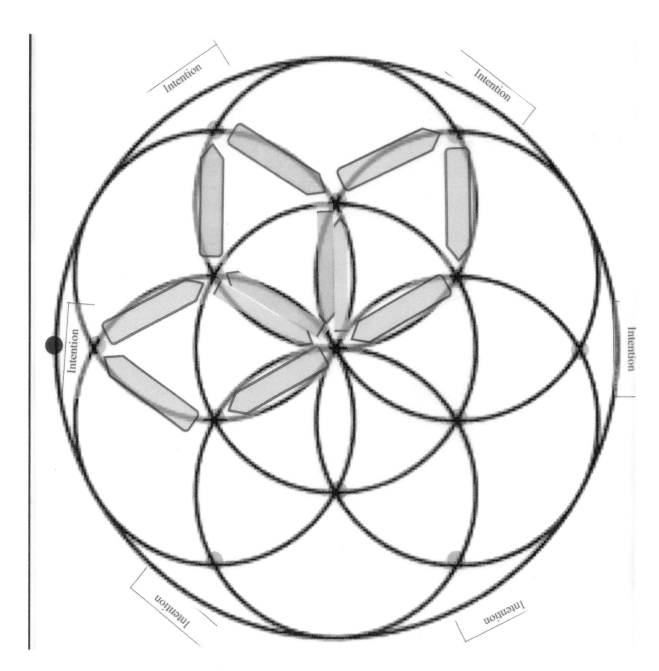

In the symbol of the flower of life is the image of the seed of life, which looks very appropriate because all flowers contain seeds. Polygonal shapes are believed to represent the feminine and some believe it is the symbol of creation. It is also said that these harmonious and interlocking circles are the blueprint of the universe.

It can be understood as representative of the various lunar cycles: increasing, full and decreasing. Sacred in various Neopagan traditions and goddesses, the Trinity of the Eye of Piscis is an ancient and powerful symbol that represents the sacred trinity and the all-seeing eye.

As a network, it can be used as an energy generator for new projects or ideas or for someone starting something new for yourself.

THE METATRON CUBE OR MERKABA

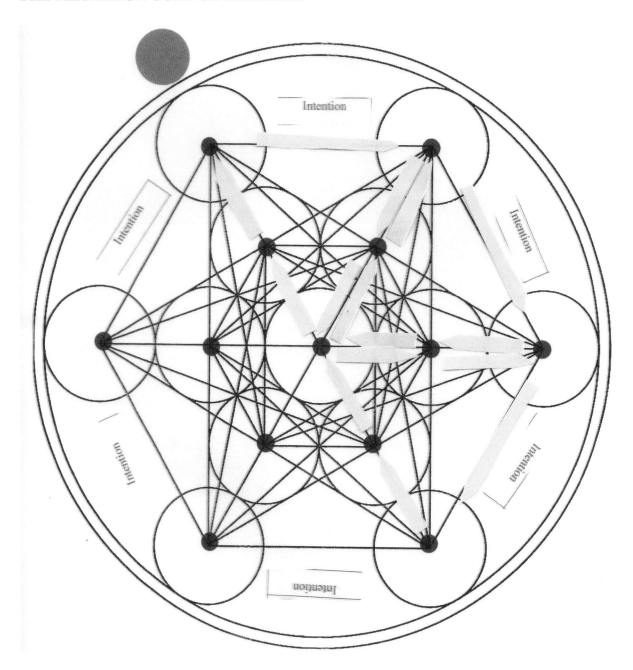

The Merkaba is another powerful symbol that is created when two star tetrahedra are combined, one pointing skyward, channeling energy from the Universe to Earth; and one pointing down, drawing energy from the Earth. The Merkaba is a light vehicle believed to be used by the ascended masters to connect and transport to the Higher Realms. "Mer" means Light. "Ka" means Spirit. "Ba" means Body.

Metatron is the archangel who is most attributed to sacred geometry and the mysteries and inner workings of the Universe. Metatron's cube is also said to symbolize the creation of life itself; the spheres represent the feminine and the straight lines connecting them represent the masculine, as they work together to create a unified whole. This powerful symbol contains the 5 Platonic solids or the 5 elements (Earth, Air, Fire, Water and Ether), and meditating on Metatron's Cube would have profound healing powers.

As a grid, it can be used for powerful healing and the development of clairsentient gifts. Any sacred geometry can be used to build a crystal grid, see star of David below:

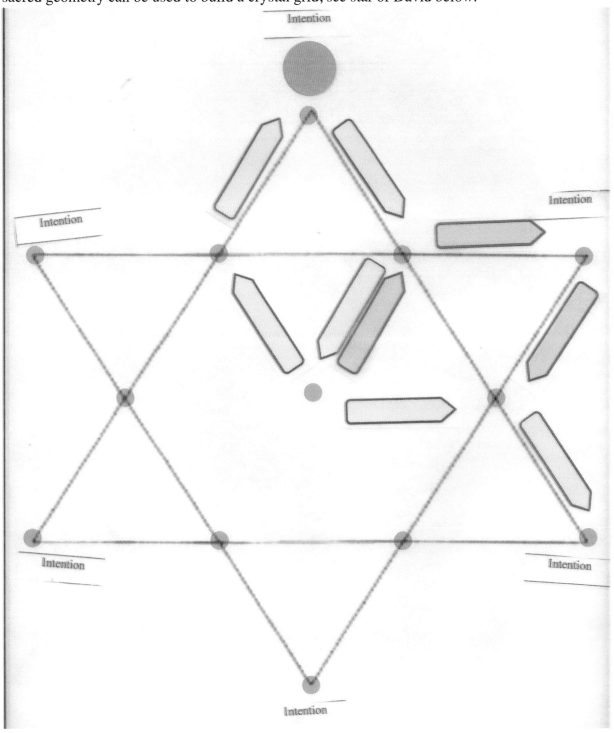

AURA CLEANING

Aura Cleansing is used when an energy is stuck in the chakras like a spider web, dusty, gray wispy thing or after a Reiki table session if the person still complains of pain in the body.

 Examples: shoulder pain, leg pain

This pain is usually caused by a problem that has long been in the person and of mental, emotional, or spiritual origin. This energy is attached to the physical body in a form of hooks, harpoons or the like and must be removed in order to relieve pain and heal the old energy wound.

This method first of all makes it possible to identify where the energy is blocked using the Byosen sweep. Once the bioke is identified, this place will be the point of entry. It is then up to the customer to identify where their physical pain is. In some cases, the pain is in the knee but the bioke was in the shoulder. This means the point of entry was in the shoulder but the person ignored the pain and the message associated with the pain for a very long time, so the pain developed branches that grew down to his knee.

This pain always contains a message. With the help of the client it is important to gain a clear image of the pain by asking questions to determine the shape, color, size, temperature, area, and solidity of the object.

The client is then asked if they are ready to release the pain. The person is expected to say yes. If she says no, there's nothing more we can do.

The client is then asked to think of the first person that comes to their mind. The client doesn't need to give us the name, just confirm that they know the person. As a master practitioner, a colour will come to mind. Ask the client to send a gentle wave of the energy of that colour to the person.

You then continue with the procedure which requires your Reiki energetic fingers. By pulling on your fingers, you lengthen the energy from 12 to 18 inches. Draw UDKM on the extended fingers and if desired, draw CKR on extended fingers. Once the fingers are extended and energized, use your middle finger to cut a slit in the identified location of the byoke large enough to accommodate the object the client has described.

Then put the backs of your hands together and press in the energetic fingers and open a space large enough for the object to pop out.

Pull out the fingers and this time with the palms of the hands together, insert the energetic fingers and allow the energy to extend and wrap around the previously described shape until it is completely covered in a cocoon of energy.

Ask your client to breathe in deeply and when exhaling gently remove the object. Take several breaths if necessary. Once the object is clear, let the object go towards the light.

Then place your hands over the opening and send Dai Ko Myo in and ask the customer how he feels now. It is possible that the pain is completely gone or a seed still remains. If some remains, simply repeat the process to remove the original seed. It is quite possible that a new person will come to the customer's mind.

When the process is complete and the client feels no more pain, draw UDKM over the area and allow the energy to heal the injury, give Reiki until your intuition tells you that the void has been filled.

You need to retract your fingers and do your closing prayer, and don't forget to dry shower.

Aura cleaning method:

a) Open prayer and send energy
b) Do a Byosen sweep
c) Find negative energy: bioke
d) Identify the problem where the pain is in the person
e) Identify the trajectory between the place of entry and the pain
f) Ask the client about pain, shape, color, size, temperature
g) Ask them if they are ready to let it go
h) Ask for the first name that comes to mind
i) What colour comes to mind of practitioner
j) The client sends the light of the colour indicated to the person who came to mind
k) Extend reiki fingers 12-18 inches
l) Draw UDKM on extended fingers
m) Optional: Draw CKR on extended fingers
n) Concentrate your intention to envelop the energy and withdraw it
o) Cut an opening to let out the object
p) With palms out, inset energetic fingers to open wide enough to take out the object
q) Insert the energetic fingers again, palms together and reach the form
r) Grab the blockage, wrap the white light around it
s) Remove dark energy slowly as the person exhales, may take several exhalations
t) Throw the object into the light as you breathe out
u) Place your hands over the opening and send Dai Ko Myo
v) Ask how the client feels
w) Repeat once to remove the seed from the client if necessary
x) Draw UDKM on the area, give REIKI
y) Fingers retracted, closing prayer and dry shower

 Opening prayer and set intent	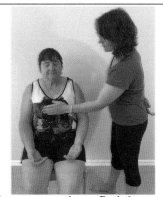 Biosen, scanning, find the negative energy: bioke.	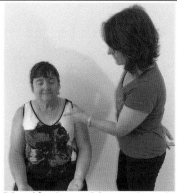 Identify the problem, where is the pain in the physical body.
 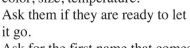 Ask the client about pain, shape, color, size, temperature. Ask them if they are ready to let it go. Ask for the first name that comes to mind. What colour comes to mind of practitioner?	 Extend reiki fingers 12-18 inches	 Draw UDKM on extended fingers Optional: Draw CKR on extended fingers
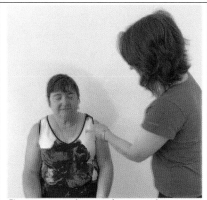 Cut an opening to let out the object	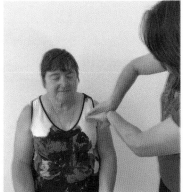 With palms out, inset energetic fingers to open wide enough to take out the object	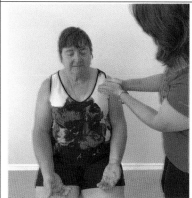 Insert the energetic fingers again, palms together and reach the form Concentrate your intention to envelop the energy .

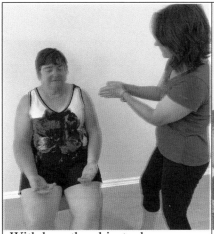		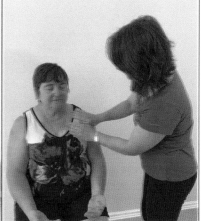
Withdraw the object when you are ready. Remove dark energy slowly as the person exhales, may take several exhalations.	Throw the object into the light as you breathe out	Place your hands over the opening and send Dai Ko Myo
	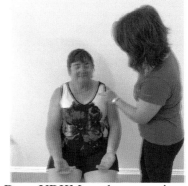	
Ask how the client feels Repeat once to remove the seed from the client if necessary	Draw UDKM on the area, give REIKI	Fingers retracted

closing prayer	Dry shower	Bioke to the light

CUTTING CORDS AND PSYCHIC LINKS

Psychic ties are energy cords that are created during our attachments in the physical world. Each meeting with various individuals forges bonds. You have connections with the bus driver, the taxi driver, the cashier at the supermarket or the waitress at the restaurant. The ropes get stronger and bulkier if the relationship becomes more important or intense as in the case of a romantic relationship or with family members.

The ropes subsequently become charged with energy each time we interact with the person and we remain tied up even though the distance between people is several kilometers. Its energies will affect us if they are not cleansed and transmuted after an encounter.

For example:

A friend meets you at the cafe and asks, "How did you choose your clothes today?" And you say "It's hot, I chose light and comfortable clothes for our hike." And the conversation naturally continues. Now imagine your mom meeting you at the same cafe at the same time for the same hike and asking, "How did you choose your clothes today?" And this time how are you feeling? Because of the psychic links, for many this question arouses insecurity, doubts, the feeling of being judged. You now feel compelled to justify your choice and yet it is the same question as before.

All of our relationships are affected in this way. We create psychic bonds with every interaction and sometimes a bond with the same person can be both positive and negative.

Negative ties hold us back in situations that are not good for us like in the case an abusive relationship, or with a person who continues turn to someone who neglects, mistreats or abuses them whether financially, physically, mentally or sexually. This can be at the level of family, friends or colleagues at work.

The ropes attach to us through the chakras. The chakras are three-dimensional energetic objects that resemble a ball so attachment can be from any direction.

By using the method of severing psychic ties, you are not going to eliminate the person from your life but rather eliminate what is negative in your relationship that is holding you in low vibration. By cleaning up these latent energies, the relationship is no longer influenced by these old energies and can develop in a positive way. It can also finally free you from a harmful relationship and give you the freedom to separate yourself from their influence.

When I did this spiritual work with the relationship I had with my mother, cutting and cleaning the ropes attached to me; I freed myself from negative emotions. When I next saw my mother, she was calmer and since I didn't have any anger or resentment towards her, we had a nice meeting. I was able to continue to have a relationship with her that improved over time.

In another case, after cutting the ropes that tied me to my boyfriend, I decided that there was no positive aspect in continuing a relationship with him and I decided to end our relationship.

You remain in control of your free will, in effect, giving yourself the power to be free to choose without being held back by old energies that affect your judgment.

In some cases, the psychic links may have been created in past lives and its links are related to Karma and the life lesson that has not been learned. The lessons of life are the goal of our incarnation on earth. It is important to examine why this situation is present in our life and what do we have to learn from it.

You can clean around a person by cutting all around, or you can take the time to examine each rope that needs to be cut one by one. Each of these ropes are created through an interaction. They may also have been created by old beliefs that prevent someone from being successful, being happy, or cause a pattern in romantic relationships. It is important to know how these psychic bonds are created so as not to recreate them again.

The client, as in the previous method, must be ready to release the ropes, he must understand and accept the lesson. The practitioner should help the client understand the lesson that is attached to the rope. Lessons are a learning process whereby a soul comes to earth to experience certain difficulties in learning, growing and evolving.

Just like the previous method, one must use the energetic fingers in order to cut the psychic links. Links can be cut before or during or after a session.

Your Reiki must first be turned on and your intention must be to cut any cords that are not for the greater good of the person.

With your client, determine a particular problem, whether emotional, physical or mental that they want to tackle. This information can also come from an energy block identified during a reiki session.

The ropes are usually black or gray, surrounded by mud, or are like roots. If you can't see, employ your intuition by using the Byosen scan. Once the situation has been identified, ask your client if they are ready to release all the ropes attached to this situation or person.

The client may need to forgive or let go of their anger. Ask clients to send white light to the situation or person. Support the client by sending Reiki.

Draw Hon Sha Za Sho Nen on the part where the psychic links are attached. You lengthen your energetic fingers like in the previous exercise and cut the ties. Be sure to cut the ties off the rope as ties are sometimes attached with hooks. Angels are really good at removing weapons and healing wounds. For more information about angels please refer to level 2 Reiki Manual.

Once the links are cut, send in the Reiki to heal the wound using UDKM.

You must also heal the other end of the rope which is also attached to a cause or a person. Remove the rope and eliminate it completely. You will imagine reproducing the same ceremony with the other person.

Repeat the Byosen scan to check for other attachments. When finished, close the session with prayer and a dry shower.

Encourage your client to pay attention to the lesson and how the connection came about in the first place.

MASSAGE TABLE SESSION

Now that we understand that the chakras are the hearts of the soul that distribute energy to the rest of the body, as does the physical heart with blood, we focus on achieving a state of greater possible relaxation and let the chakras distribute the Reiki energy through the body to all the different organs, tissues and cells to obtain a complete balance of the whole body. For this reason, the client is kept lying on his back during the entire session.

Since energy can come from the Source, wherever it is, through us and be transferred to the client, then you have to have faith that the energy can then go where it is expected. The ego has no role in Reiki sessions. We only need to focus and give our attention to giving Reiki. In doing that, the best of us is given during the session without the ego getting involved.

The part of us that is the ego shows when we take credit for the client's well-being. It is not us who perform the healing, but Reiki according to the divine will. We are no more than the wire that connects your phone to the wall outlet. The power outlet (the source) brings electricity to the outlet. Electricity is Reiki, it is present but to have access to it you have to connect. Once you connect you can recharge your batteries or help another person to recharge. Just as a wire can recharge multiple electronic devices.

REIKI ON A TABLE

Before you start, you have to wash your hands and light a candle, which represents the light of Reiki. For a session of about one hour, you can spend up to 4 minutes on the first 5 positions of the hands and then about 3 minutes for the other positions. This is of course a suggestion and not an obligation. Intuitively you may feel the need to spend more time in certain places.

One way to use symbols during a session is to introduce a symbol that comes to mind through intuition although I always encourage my students to place each symbol at each hand position. In this way we use CKR to clean up energy blockages and suck debris out of the body. Then with SHK we cleanse the mental and emotional bodies through chakras. Then we deposit a golden light with the symbol HSZSN which connects to our etheric body to release the old energies, that from previous lives and karma for a greater cleansing of the unbalanced energies, promoting a complete rejuvenation of the entire body.

If you skip a step, it doesn't matter you can go back and do the position you forgot. I see most of the variations when people go to the hips instead of the shoulders. But as soon as you remember your omission you can correct it.

The client is lying on the table ON THEIR BACK:

a) Ask the client for permission to touch him and that he accepts the energy.

b) Call in Reiki with your opening prayer, feel the Reiki connections and let yourself be the channel. See the energy flowing through your head and your hands. Ask the energy to flow for a session for (name of the person) for their greater good.

c) Do a Byosen scan to detect the byoke. See if you can feel where the energy is weakened or weakening. I prefer to do it with one hand, it is also possible to use both hands.

d) Stand at the client's crown and begin the session.

1. Hands over the eyes (Third Eye Chakra).

    i. Draw Cho Ku Rei, say the name 3 times and give for about 1 minute
    ii. Draw Sei Hi Ki, say the name 3 times and give for about 1 minute
    iii. Draw Hon Sha Ze Sho Nen, say the name 3 times and give for about 1 minute
    iv. Draw Dai Ko Myo, say the name 3 times and give for about 1 minute
    Repeat this for the next 4 chakras

2 .Put the hands on each side of the head to the ears. (Throat Chakra, listening aspect in communication)

3. Roll their head gently and put your hands underneath, cup their head in your hands and make sure your fingers line up with the occipital ridge, where the base of the skull meets the nervous system. (Manifestation Chakra)

4. Above the head: Hold your hands above the crown, making sure to cover both sides of the brain. (Crown Chakra)

5. Throat, place hands gently in front of throat, directing energy toward the Adams apple. Be sure that if the client opens their eyes, they will be able to see your hands. (Throat Chakra, aspect of expression)

Now you will draw each symbol, say the name 3 times and give for about 45 seconds

6. Place your hands below their throat, towards the top of their chest. (The Chakra of Universal Love)

7. Place your hands in the center of the chest at heart height. Leave enough space in case the client takes a deep breath so as not to touch the chest. (The Chakra of Unconditional Love)

8. Place your hands above their stomach. (Solar Plexus Chakra)

9. Place your hands above the navel. (Sacral Chakra)

10. Place your hands at the pubic area, leaving a space of almost 15-20 centimeters between your hands and the client's body. (Base Chakra)

11. Place one hand on the shoulder and the other on the hand on the side where you are already. (Chakras of the Hands) You can also choose to do the shoulders together; the best position is behind the head instead of being along side of them.

12. Place one hand on the hip and the other on the knee (or just the hips, however this is a very difficult position to do and students tend to stretch to try to cover the opposite hip. I find that doing the hip and knee on one side at a time is much simpler.) This position helps to cleanse the Karmic energies stored in the hips, legs and ankles.

13. Go to the foot of the table and put your hands above the feet. (Root Chakra).

14. On the other side of the body, place one hand on their hip and the other on their knee. (or just their knees if you've done the hips together before)

15. Place one hand on the second shoulder and the other on the hand. (Chakras of the Hands)

16. Back to the head, and now we are going to cleanse the central channel and activate the Kundalini:

17. Place the hands above the eyes again (3rd eye) and imagine Cho Ku Rei taking the elevator from the higher self and descending into the central channel connecting to all the chakras as it passes. At the Base chakra, Cho Ku Rei splits and descends down the legs and then re-enters the earth and connects to the core of the earth. You can feel the connection being made. Then the Cho Ku Rei returns up to the foot and comes back to the base chakra where it meets and enters the Kundalini channel and goes up through each chakra to the crown where Cho Ku Rei disperses in the client's aura.

18. Place the hands on either side of the head (the ears) and imagine Sei Hi Ki taking the elevator from the higher self and descending into the central channel connecting to all of the chakras as it passes. At the Base chakra, Sei Hi Ki splits and descends down the legs and then goes to a water source. Depending on the person this can be ocean, lake, river, etc. You can feel the connection being made and then Sei Hi Ki comes back to the feet and goes up to the base chakra where it meets and enters the Kundalini channel and goes up through each chakra to the crown where Sei Hi Ki disperses in the client's aura.

19. Behind the head in the same way as at the beginning, gently rock the head to each side and then put the hands below. (Manifestation Chakra) and imagine Hon Sha Ze Sho Nen taking the elevator from the higher self and descending into the central channel connecting to all of the chakras as it passes. At the Base chakra, Hon Sha Ze Sho Nen splits and descends down the legs and then connects with the breeze, a gentle wind. You can feel the connection being made and then Hon Sha Ze Sho Nen comes back up to the feet and goes up to the base chakra where it meets and enters the Kundalini channel and goes up through each chakra to the crown where Hon Sha Ze Sho Nen disperses in the client's aura.

20. Place the hands on the top of the head (Crown chakra) and imagine Dai Ko Myo taking the elevator from the higher self and descending into the central channel connecting to all the chakras as it passes. At the Base chakra, Dai Ko Myo splits and descends down the legs and then connects to the higher self through the ether. You can feel the connection being made and then Dai Ko Myo comes back up to the feet and goes up to the base chakra where it meets and enters the Kundalini channel and goes up through each chakra to the crown where Dai Ko Myo disperses in the client's aura.

21. Sweep the auric bodies.

> 21.1) 2 inches Emotional Body and send to light or candle.

> 21.2) 4 inches Mental Body and send to light or candle.

> 21.3) 6 inches Spiritual Body and send to light or candle.

Conclusion : Stand at the head of the client.

22. Make the infinity sign (8) in your left hand.

23. Gently place your hand with the sign on the top of their head where the crown chakra is located while holding the other hand on your heart and, with the intention clear in your mind, close and seal the energy to inside the aura. Hold your hand there until you feel the crown has been closed and sealed.

24. Prayer of thanks for the energy of Reiki and the Source.

25. Unplug, wipe with a dry shower.

26. Send the energy to the light or a candle.

> **Optional:** redo a scan to see if there has been a change in the client's aura / energy field with the Byosen technique or use a pendulum.

Tell the client that the session is over. Ask them to lie on the table for a few minutes, then sit up slowly and always give them a glass of water. Water after a session is beneficial and helps bring them back to the present moment.

The above positions are a reference for you when you start practicing Reiki. We are intuitive beings so I encourage you to "listen" to your internal voice. If you feel the urge to place your hands in different positions, then do so and hold the positions as long as you feel the need or as long as the energy flows intensely. Work with your intuition and trust it.

By using the symbols this way, you will learn them very quickly and begin to perceive the different energies relating to each symbol.

The elevator and return of energy through the Kundalini and dispersal of energy in the aura.

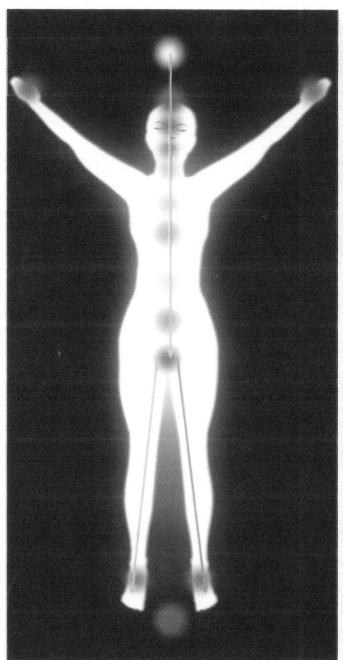

The symbols descend in a straight line

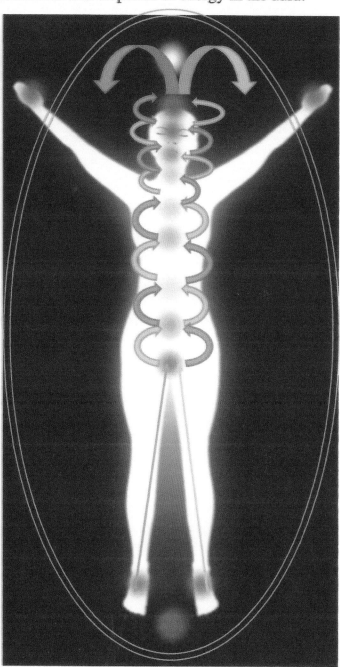

The symbols return through the Kundalini and cross at each chakra and disperse in the aura (green circle).

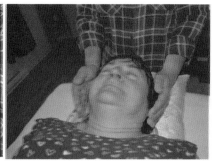

Opening prayer   1.Hands above the eyes   2. Hands over the ears

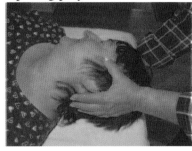
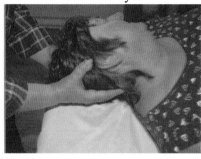

Rotate the head from left to right to put your hands under the head   3. Place the hands under the head

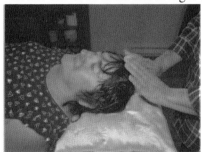
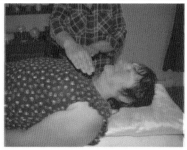

4.Hands above the crown   5. Hands above the throat   6. Hands above the chest

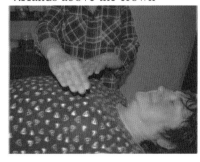
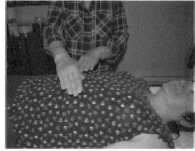
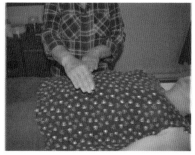

7. Hands above the heart   8. Hands above the solar plexus   9. hands above the sarcal

10. hands above the base

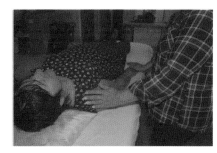

11. Hands above the shoulder and hand

12. Hands above the hip and knee

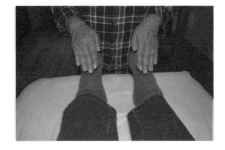

13. Hands above the feet

14. Hands above the hip and knee

15. Hands above the shoulder and hand

16. Return to the head

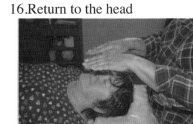

17. Hands above the eyes and Cho Ku Rei in the elevator and up the kundalini

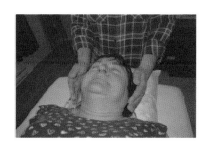

18. Hands over the ears and Sei Hi Ki in the elevator and up the kundalini

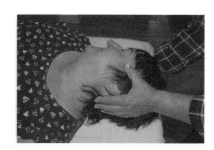

19. Rotate the head from left to right to put your hands under the head

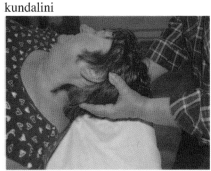

Place the hands under the head and HSZSN in the elevator and up the Kundalini

20. Hands above the crown and Dai Ko Myo in the elevator and up the Kundalini

  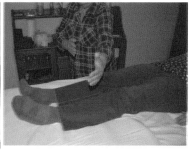

| 21.1 Sweep Emotional body | 21.2. Sweep Mental body | 21.3 Sweep Spiritual body |

| 22. Draw 8 (infinity) in the hand. | 23. Hands over crown/heart | 24. Closing prayer |

 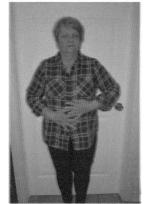 

25. Dry shower and disconnect from client

26. Send the Byosen towards the light or a candle

Do not forget that during a session you are also receiving Reiki energy and therefore you also need to clear your Auric field from all the energy that's been freed from your 5 bodies. It's important to clear your own bubble each time you give Reiki.

WORKING AS A PRACTITIONER

You can give Reiki to other people and get paid, although I always recommend that my students do a minimum of 24 free case studies before starting to charge for sessions to master the technique and to have experienced many different situations with different clients.

I recommend that you find 24 different people. Why? Because after doing 4 free sessions on one person, my students find it difficult to get paid for the fifth visit. In addition, if you are trying to establish yourself as a professional, the promotion of your services is mainly by word of mouth. The more people you have cared for, the more effective the results will be. It is also a best practice to work with different people who have different health problems or who are having different emotional and / or mental blockages to gain experience during your practice.

Even if you do not plan to join the association, complete the form after each session in case you change your mind. Many of my students regret not having followed this advice and more than 24 case studies had to be completed in order to join the association at a later date. You never know what the future holds, it is better to be considerate and other than the cost of 24 photocopies, this gives you a benchmark for noticing your progress as a practitioner.

The price for a Level 2 student for one-hour session should be between $40 and $50 dollars depending on your experience and whether or not you have to travel. There should always be an exchange for Reiki and during your 24-case studies people will complete the form as their part of the exchange. As you gain experience, you can accept an exchange of care instead of a cash payment if you wish.

Your first investment should be a massage table. You do not need to buy a new one because you can put a sheet on the table. There are regularly massage tables for sale in Facebook, Craigslist or Kijiji spaces for less than in stores.

At first, I worked at people's homes because I had no space for a massage table. Then I vacated a bedroom and gave care in that room. You can also rent a room in an office that offers massages or chiropractic care.

MARKETING

In the beginning, your practice will be word of mouth. It is important to have business cards so that people can contact you. Be confident and tell everyone about your Reiki practice. Advertise it on social media, putting your diploma on Pintrest or Instagram are simple examples that convey a clear message. I am a practitioner and I am open to the public! In Canada, the standards of practice are precise. If you are offering Reiki, you must simply offer only Reiki during your session. You can make use of promotional offers such as the tenth session is free or a 25% discount if someone refers a new customer to you.

Fairs are a great place to get known in the area and is a good way to demonstrate an example of a chair session for 10-15-minutes.

Schools or charities sometimes have silent auctions. You can have a gift certificate that people can bid on. Leave several cards on the table so that interested people who don't win the bid can still contact you.

You can volunteer in hospitals, care facilities for the elderly, or charity events to make yourself known to other groups. They can learn about Reiki and may invite you to practice in those environments.

During all these events, try to get a contact list (name, phone, email) of people who have expressed an interest in Reiki. You can use it if you are having an open house party or a free Reiki evening.

After all my years promoting Reiki, my courses and my Institute, I find that the costs are not directly proportional to the results. If you think spending a lot of money is going to be successful, well, that's not always the case. Renting an office instead of practicing at home may not be the best idea. Provide quality service and people will hear about you and contact you.

A presence on the internet is very useful. It allows you to be on a website as a practitioner in your area and also helps to generate a clientele.

In some cities it is necessary to have an operating license and to obtain it you must be a member of the association. It is prudent to have liability insurance in the event of an accident which you can obtain from the association or a private firm.

If you have the space to dedicate a room to Reiki sessions, a nice complement to Reiki are crystals or aromatherapy. Some people are very particular and sensitive to scents so before burning sage or incense ask your client what their preferences are. You will need one or more candles and soft, instrumental music to fill the silence of the session. I always use the same CD so I know where I am in the span of my session and whether I should slow down or go faster.

You will need to have a place to keep client records confidential.

If you receive payments you can now enter the expenses associated with your Reiki practice for tax purposes. It is important to keep all of your receipts.

OTHER LEVELS OF REIKI

In the Usui system, there are four levels. Although some teachers combine the level of Master Practitioner and that of Master Teacher for a total of three levels. In my training, I use the traditional Usui symbols and also the Tibetan symbols and those of the sacred fire as well as those which relate to the Universal Spiritual Reiki.

I give my students the choice to learn the style they prefer so I teach the Master Practitioner Level separate from the Master Teacher Level. Until this point the three approaches are exactly the same for the first three levels which are the original basic techniques of Mikao Usui.

At Reiki I Level, you receive an attunement and learn to use the energy of Reiki for practical sessions, both to heal yourself and to heal others. It opens the channels of the body for Reiki to flow, connecting you to the Divine Source at a higher level than if you just need meditation. Once attuned, you are always open.

At Reiki II Level, you receive three of the sacred symbols and additional initiations that allow you to perform Reiki from a distance, as well as in the future and the past. You learn to use your intuition more and to feel the direction of the Divine Source. Level II Reiki provides higher vibrational energy and a stronger Reiki connection, bringing increased sensitivity and intuitive awareness.

At Reiki III Level, you receive master training and tools. At this level, you receive the fourth of the four sacred Usui symbols, the Master Usui symbol, and an attunement with this energy. You will also receive additional Reiki tools like the crystal grid and aura surgery. At this point, new growth is inevitable and the individual will benefit from this growth. Changes will have already taken place in the 6 month wait period between level 1-2 and level 3 and the learning curve will be much greater.

At the Master Teacher Level,

A) If you choose the path of Universal Spiritual Reiki, you receive the symbol of the trinity and training in breathing which will give you the ability to teach and transmit Reiki initiations to others. You will learn to give self-initiations, psychic attunements and healing attunements. It is important to be clear that the initiation to the Reiki Master does not make anyone a guru, but rather a master of himself and a commitment to undertake and evolve towards this state.

This method respects the Tibetan and shamanic method but the initiation of the students is less complicated and students who had originally been attuned in the Tibetan way have felt great changes. Measures taken with their Reiki before and after note an amplification of the possibility of channeling and their clients notice an amplification of the energy received during the session.

B) If you choose the Tibetan way you receive the Tibetan master symbol and the breathing training which will give you the ability to teach and transmit Reiki initiations to others. You will learn to give self-initiations, psychic attunements and healing attunements. It is important to be clear that the initiation to Reiki Master does not make anyone a guru, but rather a master of himself and a commitment to undertake and evolve towards this state.

AUTHOR SONYA ROY

Sonya received her Reiki 1 training in Vancouver in 2012 from Chrysta-Lynn. She continued her Reiki level 2 training in Vancouver in 2013 with Chrysta-Lynn. She received her Master Practitioner training from Gail Thackray in Vancouver in 2013 and then her Master Teacher training from Merrie Baker.

In 2015, she created a Shamanic Reiki course based on her grandmother's teaching. During her Reiki initiation at level 2, she had a vision of Master Mikao Usui who gave her the long-distance symbol for long distance reiki HSZSN. She continued her training with Karuna Reiki and Holy Fire® in Hawaii in 2016 with William Rand.

Sonya was already practicing energy healing as her grandmother Marie Jeanne Laniel-Desrosiers had taught her at the age of 14. She published her spiritual transformation in her book called I Dragon: Biography of a Spiritual Transformation.

She founded the Redu Wellness Center in Vancouver in 2013 and started offering energy healing sessions and giving reiki classes and other shamanic training. In 2017, she opened the Institut de la Conscience Éveillée in Québec and now offers classes in French and English in Canada, the United-States, Europe and South America.

Sonya Roy *Learning Reiki is passed from Master to student. Lineage shows what reiki masters learned from who in a direct line – bringing back to the original founder Master Usui. This is my Usui/Tibetan and Holy Fire lineage.*

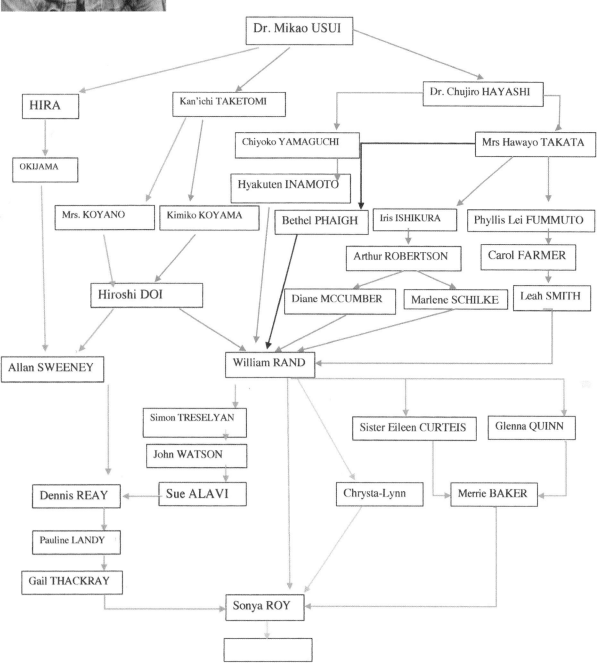

References

13 chakra system of ancient Egypt, by Sonya Roy, REDU wellness center publishing, 2018

La bible du Reiki,3ᵉ édition de Éléanor McKenzie aux Éditions Tredaniel , 2016

Class notes from Christa-Lynn, 2012-2013

Class notes from Merrie Baker Master Teacher, 2013

Essential Reiki : a complete guide to an ancient healing art by Diane Stein , the crossing press 1995

I, dragon : biography of a spiritual transformation by Sonya Roy, REDU wellness center publishing, 2019

The Lost Steps of Reiki: The Channeled Messages of Wei Chi, de Kevin Ross Emery and Thomas A. Hensel, light lines publishing, 1 mai 1997.

Reiki Shamanism: A guide to out-of-body healing by Jim Pathfinder Ewing, Findhorn Press, 2008

Reiki: the healing touch; 1ˢᵗ and 2ⁿᵈ degree manual updated edition by William Rand , Vision publications 2008

Reiki Usui & Tibetan level 1 certification manual: Energy healing for beginners by Gail Thackray, Indian Spring Publishing, 2012

Reiki Usui & Tibetan level 2 certification manual: Practitioner level energy healing by Gail Thackray, Indian Spring Publishing, 2012

Sacred Flames Reiki by Allison Dalhaus a.k.a. Dharmadevi, Reiki Blessings Press, 2002

Télos 1 Revelations of the new Lemuria, Aurélia Louise Jones, Mount Shasta light publishing, 2004

Télos 2 Messages for the enlightenment of a humanity in Transformation, Aurélia Louise Jones, Mount Shasta light publishing, 2004

Télos 3 Protocols for the fifth dimension, Aurélia Louise Jones, Mount Shasta light publishing, 2006

You can heal your life, Louise Hay , Hay House, 1999

Printed in Great Britain
by Amazon

27434281R00037